SUBMARINES
of
The Royal Navy

SUBMARINES OF THE ROYAL NAVY

Throughout history, sea power has proved a deciding factor in the ambitions of one country over another — and still does today.

And the deciding factor in sea power today is most likely to be the submarine.

Submarines can dive deep and stay deep — away from the highly dangerous surface of the sea, where vessels are easily located by aircraft or satellites and are increasingly vulnerable to long-range missile attack. New knowledge of temperature and salinity layers in the oceans, which can conceal the submarine against the probing sensors of ships and aircraft, has created an underwater jungle for the submarine commander to exploit like a tiger in the shadows.

The Royal Navy's Submarine Flotilla is a carefully balanced force which, together with surface and airborne units of the Royal Navy and Royal Air Force and combined with NATO forces, provides a complete mix to counter a variety of maritime threats.

SUBMARINE TYPES

The Submarine Flotilla of the Royal Navy is currently the only arm of the Service which is expanding.

There are three basic types of submarine operated by the Royal Navy; each with a specialist role to play. These are the nuclear-powered FLEET submarine; the nuclear-powered POLARIS submarine and the diesel-electric powered PATROL submarine.

At present the Royal Navy has 33 submarines — eleven Fleet, four Polaris and sixteen Patrol boats. Two other Fleet submarines of the new and improved type are under construction, to be known as the Trafalgar class.

FLEET SUBMARINES

HM Submarines DREADNOUGHT, VALIANT, WARSPITE, CHURCHILL, CONQUEROR, COURAGEOUS, SWIFTSURE, SOVEREIGN, SUPERB, SCEPTRE, SPARTAN, SPLENDID, TRAFALGAR, and TURBULENT.

The Fleet submarine is the modern equivalent of the battleship. It is the main striking power of the Fleet and the single most effective anti-submarine weapon available to the maritime commander.

Its main role is to seek and destroy enemy submarines and surface ships in wartime. It is also capable of conducting ocean-wide covert surveillance.

A Fleet submarine is about 280 feet long and displaces 4,500 tons when dived. It has a crew of about 110.

It is nuclear-powered. A small nuclear reactor provides heat to produce steam and the steam drives turbine machinery which will propel the submarine at speeds greater than 25 knots at depths in excess of 500 feet.

Fresh water is distilled from seawater and a small amount of fresh water is electrolysed to produce oxygen and hydrogen. The hydrogen is eliminated and the oxygen replenishes the "closed" atmosphere of the submarine. Waste and noxious gases are eliminated to keep the atmosphere pure. The steam turbines also produce massive amounts of electrical power — enough to meet the needs of a small town. This enables the use of a vast array of sensors, computers and navigational equipment. Using sonar the submarine is able to identify possible targets and other ships by identifying the noise signatures made.

Submarine targets can be engaged by the Tigerfish wire-guided homing torpedo (soon to be given an anti-surface ship capability) and surface targets can be engaged with salvo (unguided) torpedoes. Fleet submarines are being equipped with Sub-Harpoon — an underwater-launched, long-range, air-flight guided missile to attack surface ships. Fired when the submarine is dived the missile is able to take off from the surface of the sea to home on an enemy surface ship many miles away. With sophisticated navigational equipment and the ability to operate at high speeds constantly — even when surface ships are battling against gales — the Fleet submarine is a formidable weapon capable of operating unaided anywhere in the world.

Once a Fleet submarine is at sea and dived it represents a dangerous series of question marks for the "other side".

Where is it? What is it doing or watching? Is it using its capability to shadow — and if it is, for what purpose? Is anything that an enemy might do at sea likely to be compromised as the result of unknown, undetected surveillance by a Fleet submarine?

There are no publishable answers to these questions, neither can there be. The existence of this sub-surface capability adds up to deterrence, however. One certain responsibilty of the Submarine Flotilla in peacetime is to train to wage war as effectively as possible in the knowledge that this will contribute to its prevention.

PROTOTYPE NUCLEAR POWERED FLEET SUBMARINE — "DREADNOUGHT"

The R.N.'s first nuclear powered submarine especially designed to hunt and destroy enemy submariners — A "hunter/killer" capable of continuous high underwater speed and endurance. Her hull was British built but her nuclear plant was made in the U.S.A. by General Dynamics Corporation. The complete nuclear reactor of the type fitted in U.S.S. Skipjack, was purchased in the U.S. to hasten Dreadnought's launch.

She was fitted with an inertial navigation system and with the means of measuring depth below ice.

The "Dreadnought" arrived at the North Pole at 0800 on 3 March, 1971, the first British submarine to do so. She had sailed 1,500 miles under the ice before surfacing at the Pole. She came to the surface at 5.30 in the evening and remained on the surface until the early hours of the next morning. Dreadnough has now (1982) been retired and is at Chatham. After she has been defuelled and de-equipped she will be placed at a secure mooring until scrapped/sunk.

Specifications

Builders	Vickers Armstrong, Barrow
Launch Date	21 October, 1960
First Commissioned	17 April, 1963
Cost	£18,455,000
Displacement (tons)	3,000 (surface) 4,000 (submerged)
Length overall	265 feet 9 inches
Beam	32 feet 3 inches
Mean draught	26 feet
Speed	30 knots
Armament	Homing torpedoes
Torpedo tubes	Six 21″ Bow - all internal
Complement	95

When **HMS DREADNOUGHT**, the Royal Navy's first nuclear-powered submarine, was laid down in 1959 she represented an evolution in naval warfare as great as the change from sail to steam.

HUNTER-KILLER — "VALIANT" CLASS

Specifications

Displacement (tons)	3,500 (surfaced); 4,500 (submerged)
Length overall	285 feet
Beam	33 feet 3 inches
Mean draught	27 feet
Speed	30 knots
Armament	Homing torpedoes
Torpedo tubes	Six 21", forward
Complement	95

NAME	BUILDER	LAUNCH DATE	FIRST COMMISSIONED	COST
Valiant	Vickers Ltd Barrow	3.12.63	18.7.66	£25,300,000
Warspite	Vickers Ltd Barrow	25.9.65	18.4.67	£21,455,000
Churchill	Vickers Ltd Barrow	20.12.68	15.7.70	£24,661,000
Conqueror	Cammell Laird Birkenhead	28.8.69	9.11.71	£29,319,000
Courageous	Vickers Ltd Barrow	7.3.70	16.10.71	£24,858,000

HMS VALIANT (above) was laid at Vickers Limited at Barrow-in-Furness on 14 June 1959. She was launched in December 1963 and completed in the summer of 1966.

On 25th April, 1967 she arrived home on completion of a 12,000 mile voyage — underwater — from Singapore. This 28 day non-stop submerged passage was a record for a British submarine.

HMS WARSPITE (right). Laid down December 1963; Launched 25 September 1965; Commissioned 18 April 1967; 4500 tons; 285 feet.

HMS CHURCHILL (above). Length 285 feet; Beam 33 feet; Displacement 3,500 tons standard. She was cast in the mould of the DREADNOUGHT, the Royal Navy's prototype nuclear submarine.

HMS CHURCHILL, the third all-British nuclear-powered Fleet submarine of the Valiant class and was launched on December 20, 1968 by the Hon. Mrs C. Soames, daughter of Sir Winston Churchill. The boat was commissioned on July 15, 1970.

HMS CONQUEROR (right) was laid down by Cammell Laird and Company at Birkenhead on December 15 1967 and first commissioned on November 9 1971. She is 285 feet long and has a displacement of 3,500 tons. Her decks are built into a pressure hull 30 feet in diameter.

During the Falklands conflict sunk the Argentinian Cruiser General Belgrano in the South Atlantic.

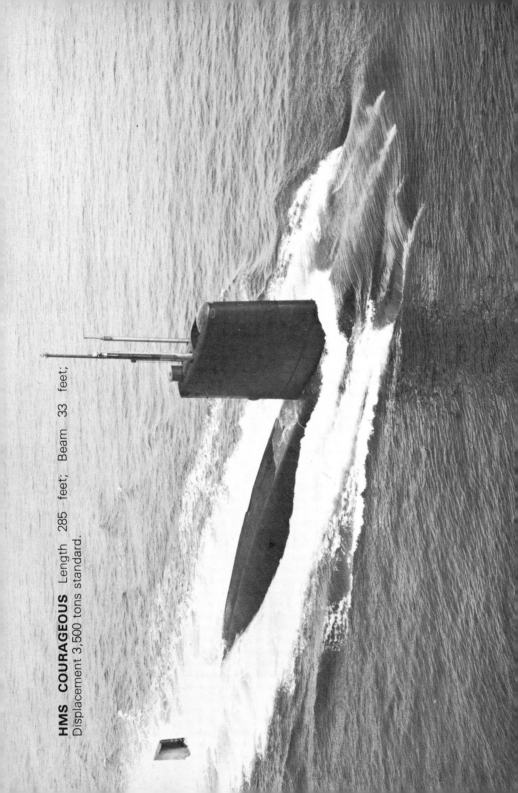

HMS COURAGEOUS Length 285 feet; Beam 33 feet; Displacement 3,500 tons standard.

"SWIFTSURE CLASS"

Similar to the "Valiant" Class, but these are slightly shorter, and have one less torpedo tube. They also have a deeper diving capability.

Specifications

Displacement (tons)	4,200 (surfaced), 4,500 (submerged)
Length overall	272 feet
Beam	32 feet 3 inches
Mean draught	27 feet
Speed	Over 30 knots submerged
Armament	Homing torpedoes
Torpedo tubes	Five 21"
Complement	97

NAME	BUILDERS	LAUNCH DATE	FIRST COMMISSIONED	COST
Swiftsure	Vickers Ltd Barrow	7.9.71	17.4.73	£35,022,000
Sovereign	Vickers Ltd Barrow	17.2.73	11.7.74	£31,067,000
Superb	Vickers Ltd Barrow	30.11.74	13.11.76	£41,300,000
Sceptre	Vickers Ltd Barrow	20.11.76	14.2.78	£43,225,000
Spartan	Vickers Ltd Barrow	7.4.78	22.9.79	£69,000,000
● **Splendid**	Vickers Ltd Barrow	5.10.79	21.3.81	£97,000,000

● Originally named "Severn" when ordered, but launched as "Splendid".

HMS SWIFTSURE (above). Length 272 feet; Beam 32 ft 2 ins; Displacement 4,400 tons.

The name Swiftsure, said to be a compound of "Swift pursuer" is one of the oldest in the Royal Navy, dating back to the reign of Eizabeth I. In fact, the Queen may have chosen it herself, as she did the name Warspite.

HMS SOVEREIGN (right). Displacement 4,400 tons; Length 272 feet; Beam 32 feet; Draught 29 feet. She was launched in February 1973 and commissioned on July 11, 1974.

In 1976 the SOVEREIGN surfaced at the North Pole after operating for at last ten days under the ice cap in the Arctic.

HMS SUPERB (above) was commissioned in November 1976 after being built at Vickers Shipbuilders, Barrow-in-Furness. Two previous HMS SUPERB's were each known in the Fleet as "Super B". The present SUPERB has adopted the "Super Bee" as its unofficial badge.

HMS SCEPTRE (right) was commissioned at Vickers Shipbuilders, Barrow-in-Furness, on 14 February 1978. She is the first of the Royal Navy's new generation of nuclear-powered submarines to be named after a previous submarine. The last SCEPTRE was a World War II S-Class submarine of 990 tons, which distinguished herself by sinking or damaging 11 enemy ships and in operations with the famous X-craft midget submarines in attacks against the German battleship Tirpitz and the floating dock at Bergen, Norway.

HMS SPARTAN (above) joined the 2nd Submarine Squadron at Devonport on December 14, 1979. She is 275 feet long and 33.2 feet in beam. She displaces 4,500 tons, has a speed of 30 knots dived and has a complement of 12 officers and 98 ratings.

HMS SPLENDID (right) is the twelfth of the type and the last of six in the Swiftsure class. She was launched at Vickers Shipbuilders, Barrow-in-Furness on October 5, 1979. HMS SPLENDID began her first commission on March 21 1981.

Modern submarines look a lot bigger out of the water, as this photograph of the launch of HMS SPLENDID shows.

POLARIS SUBMARINES

HM Submarines RESOLUTION, RENOWN, REPULSE and REVENGE.

Polaris submarines are strategic weapons. They form Britain's contribution to the NATO strategic deterrent.

They are nuclear-powered and are similar to the Fleet submarines except that they have an extra compartment amidships which houses sixteen A-3 Polaris inter-continental ballistic nuclear missiles.

Polaris submarines are 425 feet long (2½ times Nelson's Column) and displace 8,500 tons. They have a crew of 147. To enable these boats to spend the maximum possible time at sea, they have two crews — one on leave or on training courses — and one at sea. At least one of these vessels is always on patrol. Each one has a fire power greater than all the explosives expended by all sides in both World Wars.

The 31-foot long missiles are fired from beneath the water. The guidance requirements for each missile are calculated by two high speed computers. To ensure that these requirements are correct, the computers check calculations to see where the missile would fall if launched and, if all is correct, fire the missile. All this within the last 30 milliseconds before firing.

Each missile is housed in its own launch tube. Prior to launch the tube would be pressurised to slightly above sea pressure. High pressure gas would then be squirted into the bottom end of the missile tube to send Polaris on its way. The only sensation experienced by the crew would be a quiet hiss and a slight vibration.

At the surface the first-stage motor would ignite. After about one minute it would burn out and first-stage separation and second-stage ignition occur. During powered flight an inertial guidance system with extremely precise gyroscopes, accelerometers and digital computer would put the missile on course, directing pitch, yaw and roll. At a pre-determined moment the guidance system would shut off the rocket motors and trigger separation of the re-entry body from the rest of the missile. The re-entry body then follows a ballistic trajectory to the target.

The missiles, manufactured in the United States and fitted with British warheads, have a range of 2,500 nautical miles (its accuracy is measured in yards). The point in the world furthest from the sea is near Lake Baikal, in Central Asia — 1,720 miles inland.

Polaris submarines spend many weeks at a time on patrol. Their job is to remain undetected and ready to fire their missiles. No advance in anti-submarine development has eroded their invulnerability.

Considerable effort has been made to make the long periods on patrol as comfortable as possible. Messes are spacious, there is a cinema with a plentiful supply of films, an excellent library and various quizzes etc., are arranged in order that the men's minds do not stagnate.

Specifications

Displacement (tons)	7,500 (surfaced); 8,400 (submerged)
Length overall	425 feet
Beam	33 feet
Mean draught	30 feet
Speed	Over 20 knots submerged
Armament	16 Polaris A-3 missiles
Torpedo tubes	Six 21″ forward
Complement	144 in each crew

NAME	BUILDER	LAUNCH DATE	FIRST COMMISSIONED	COST
Resolution	Vickers Ltd Barrow	15.9.66	30.10.67	£40,240,000
Renown	Cammell Laird Birkenhead	25.2.67	11.68	£39,950,000
Repulse	Vickers Ltd Barrow	4.11.67	28.9.68	£37,500,000
Revenge	Cammell Laird Birkenhead	15.3.68	4.12.69	£38,000,000

HMS RESOLUTION (above) was the first of the Royal Navy's nuclear-powered Polaris submarines to enter service, built by Vickers-Armstrong at Barrow-in-Furness. She was laid down on February 26, 1964 and launched on September 15, 1966, by Queen Elizabeth, the Queen Mother. Sea trials started in June 1967, and she was commissioned on October 2 of the same year. Early in 1968 HMS RESOLUTION sailed for American waters, making her first — and successful — firing of the Polaris guided missile on February 15, 1968. She started her operation life in June 1968.

HMS RENOWN (right) was the third Royal Navy Polaris submarine to enter service. Built by Cammell Laird's, Birkenhead, she was launched on February 25, 1967 and commissioned in November, 1968. HMS RENOWN is 425 feet long and displaces 8,500 tons.

HMS REPULSE (above) was built by Vickers-Armstrong at Barrow-in-Furness. She was launched on November 4, 1967, and commissioned a year later.

Polaris submarines spend many weeks at a time on patrol — at least one is *always* on patrol. Their job is to remain undetected and ready to fire their missiles. No advance in anti-submarine development has eroded their invulnerability.

HMS REVENGE (right) was built by Cammell Laird at Birkenhead and launched in March 1968. Commissioned on December 4, 1969, she fired her first test missile down the Eastern Atlantic test range off the Florida coast in June 1970 and began her first patrol in September that year.

PATROL SUBMARINES (Oberon Class)

Hm Submarines ORPHEUS, OBERON, ODIN, OLYMPUS, ONSLAUGHT, OTTER, ORACLE, OTUS, OSIRIS, OCELOT, OPOSSUM, OPPORTUNE, ONYX.

Oberon Class Patrol submarines are 295 feet long, have a beam of 26 feet, displace 1,610 tons, and have a crew of seven officers and sixty-two ratings.

When submerged they displace 2,410 tons and rely on batteries to drive the main motors, which give them an underwater speed in excess of 15 knots. Diesel generators recharge the batteries periodically. To reduce the possibility of detection, the air for the diesel engines can be drawn down through a snort system while the submarine remains submerged. By this means the submarine can remain dived for periods of more than six weeks.

In spite of modern developments in underwater detection equipment, the sea itself affords the submarines excellent cover from which it can strike without warning. This element of surprise, coupled with her ability to hide beneath the waves, makes the Oberon Class submarine eminently suitable for her main wartime role of seeking and destroying enemy surface ships and submarines. She can also be used to land reconaissance parties on the enemy shore. The main armament consists of three types of torpedoes, including homing torpedoes. These can be fired through any of the eight torpedo tubes. Twenty torpedoes can be carried for the six bow tubes and another four for the two stern tubes.

In peacetime their role includes the training of warships in the detection and destruction of submarines by acting as targets, though the role is often reversed to give the submarines opportunity to practice their attacks. The submarines also exercise with maritime aircraft tracking other submarines.

Each crew member attends a specialist training school for 6 weeks followed by 3 months at sea. Then, if he passes the examination, he becomes a qualified submariner and is entitled to wear the submarine badge.

Specifications
**OBERON
CLASS**

Displacement (tons)	1,610 (surfaced); 2,410 (submerged)
Length overall	295 feet
Beam	26 feet
Mean Draught	18 feet
Speed	15 knots + (12 knots dived)
Armament	Homing Torpedoes
Torpedo tubes	6 forward, 2 stern
Complement	69

NAME	BUILDER	LAUNCH DATE	FIRST COMMISSIONED
Oberon	HM Dockyard Chatham	18.7.59	24.2.61
Odin	Cammell Laird Birkenhead	4.11.60	3.5.62
Orpheus	Vickers Ltd, Barrow	17.11.59	25.11.60
Olympus	Vickers Ltd, Barrow	14.6.61	7.7.62
Osiris	Vickers Ltd, Barrow	29.11.62	11.1.64
Onslaught	HM Dockyard Chatham	24.9.60	14.8.62
Otter	Scotts, Greenock	15.5.61	20.8.62

Specifications

**OBERON
CLASS**

NAME	BUILDER	LAUNCH DATE	FIRST COMMISSIONED
Oracle	Cammell Laird Birkenhead	26.9.61	14.2.63
Ocelot	HM Dockyard Chatham	5.5.62	31.1.64
Otus	Scotts - Greenock	17.10.62	5.10.63
Opossum	Cammel Laird Birkenhead	23.5.63	5.6.64
Opportune	Scotts - Greenock	14.2.64	29.12.64
Onyx	Cammel Laird Birkenhead	18.8.66	20.11.67

HMS OBERON (right) was first commissioned at Chatham Dockyard on February 9, 1961. She is 295 feet long, displaces 2,400 tons dived and has a crew of 69.

HMS ODIN (above) is 295 feet long, displaces 2,400 tons dived and has a crew of 69. She was built by Cammell Laird & Co. Ltd., at Birkenhead and commissioned in April 1962. She is the Royal Navy's sixth HMS ODIN — named after the ruler of the mythological Norse gods — see photo!!

HMS ORPHEUS (right) was built by Vickers-Armstrong and commissioned the first of her class in 1960.

HMS OSIRIS (above) is 295 feet long, displaces 2,400 tons dived and has a crew of 69. Built by Vickers-Armstrong Ltd., she was laid down in January 1962 and launched the following November, being first commissioned in 1964.

HMS OLYMPUS (right) was launced in June 1961 and completed in July 1962.

HMS ONSLAUGHT (above) was the first submarine to bear the name in the Royal Navy. She was built by HM Dockyard, Chatham and launched in September 1960.

HMS OTTER (right) was built by Scotts S & E Ltd. of Greenock and first commissioned in August 1962. She was re-commissioned on 14 March 1973 at Cammell Lairds, Birkenhead after the first contract refit of a submarine for 15 years.

HMS ORACLE (above) was built by Cammell Lairds Shipyard at Birkenhead. She was first commissioned on February 14, 1963.

The submarine is affiliated to Old Moore's Almanac, who presented her with a crystal ball as a token of friendship between the two "Oracles".

HMS OCELOT (right) was the first of her name to serve with the Royal Navy. Built at HM Dockyard, Chatham, she was laid down in November 1960, launched in May 1962 and completed in January 1964.

HMS OTUS (above) These are generally regaded as the finest conventional submarines in the world and are also operated by Australia, Canada, Brazil and Chile.

HMS OTUS was built by Scotts of Greenock and was laid down in May 1961. She was launched the following year and her first commission started on October 5, 1963.

HMS OPOSSUM (right) was launched in 1963. She was the last conventional submarine to be refitted at Chatham, marking the end of a 60-year link between the Dockyard and non-nuclear-powered submarines.

HMS OPPORTUNE (above) was build at Greenock in 1964 and is the third Royal Navy vessel to bear the name.

HMS ONYX (right) was laid down at Cammell Lairds at Birkenhead in November 1964 and was completed three years later.

PATROL SUBMARINES (Porpoise Class)

HM Submarines PORPOISE, WALRUS, SEALION.

The Porpoise Class submarines were the forerunners of the Oberon Class, and are of virtually the same design and content. They have been modernised. Porpoise class submarines displace 1,605 tons standard and 2,405 tons submerged. They are 295 feet long and have eight 21-inch torpedo tubes: six bow and two stern. They are complemented by six officers and 65 ratings.

Living conditions are of the highest standards, in both 'O' and 'P' classes, with air conditioning for either arctic or tropical waters. Oxygen replenishment and carbon monoxide elimination to make it possible to remain totally submerged without the use of snort apparatus for several days. Distilling equipment produces fresh water from the sea.

Like the 'O' Class submarine, this class is powered by two diesel-electric sets, each driven by an Admiralty Standard Range 16 cylinder diesel. Electric motors drive two shafts giving a speed of more than 15 knots when submerged. Ability to remain submerged for several weeks: high underwater silent speed, well proved and efficient control systems, and the most up to date sonar (underwater detection equipment) make these submarines formidable adversaries.

All British submarines are fitted with high definition radar, principally for use as an aid to navigation in confined waters or poor visibility. They are also fitted with interception equipment which enables them to detect the searching radar pulses from enemy ships or aircraft in time to avoid detection by going deep. Porpoise submarines are armed with homing torpedoes and have a large reload capacity. They will eventually be replaced by the new Type 2400 conventional submarine long awaited by the Navy.

Specifications

Displacement (tons)	1,605 (surfaced); 2,405 (submerged)
Length overall	259 feet
Beam	26 feet
Mean draught	18 feet
Speed	15 knots + (12 knots dived)
Armament	Homing Torpedoes
Torpedo tubes	Six 21″ forward; two 21″ stern
Complement	71

NAME	BUILDER	LAUNCH DATE	FIRST COMMISSIONED	COST
Porpoise	Vickers - Barrow Barrow	25.4.56	17.4.58	
Sealion	Cammel Laird Birkenhead	31.12.59	25.7.61	
Walrus	Scotts Greenock	22.9.59.	10.2.61	

HMS Finwhale of this class is used as a 'non-seagoing' training ship at HMS Dolphin, Gosport.

HMS PORPOISE (above) was laid down on 15 June 1954, launched on 25 April 1956 and commissioned two years later on 17 April 1958. She was withdrawn from service in mid 1982 pending a decision on her future.

HMS SEALION (right) is 295 feet long, displaces 2,400 tons dived and has a crew of 71. The second submarine to bear the name in the Royal Navy, she was built by Cammell Laird at Birkenhead and launched on December 31, 1959.

HMS WALRUS — Length 295 feet; Beam 26.5 feet; Displacement 2,030 tons. She was launched at Scotts Yard on the Clyde by HRH The Duchess of Gloucester in 1959, and was first commissioned in February 1961.

THE WAY AHEAD . . .

TRIDENT — Successor to Polaris

The four Polaris submarines will come to the end of their service in the mid-1990's. They will be replaced by a new fleet of submarines designed to carry the American Trident C-4 rocket with a British warhead.

The £5,000m project — most of which will be spent in British shipyards and factories — will allow Britain to maintain an independent nuclear deterrent committed to the NATO Alliance.

Like HMS Resolution, HMS Renown, HMS Repulse, and HMS Revenge, each of the new submarines will carry 16 solid-fuel intercontinental ballistic missiles. Trident missiles, however, far exceed Polaris's capability. Each has eight independently targetted warheads and is three-stage, with a range of 4,000 miles, compared with the Polaris maximum of 2,800 miles (nowhere in the world is more than 1,700 miles from the sea).

In a world where nuclear weapons cannot be 'disinvented' it is the United Kingdom's surest way of preserving peace.

The American weapons system has been in operation in the United States since 1979. In Britain, as well as the building of the submarines, warheads and support equipment, the Trident programme will involve new construction projects at the Coulport armament depot and the Clyde Submarine Base at Faslane, Scotland.

TRAFALGAR CLASS FLEET SUBMARINES

The first of the 'improved Swiftsure' class of Fleet Submarines, HMS Trafalgar was launched at Barrow-in-Furness early in 1981. The second, now building, will be named HMS Turbulent and two more, have been ordered.

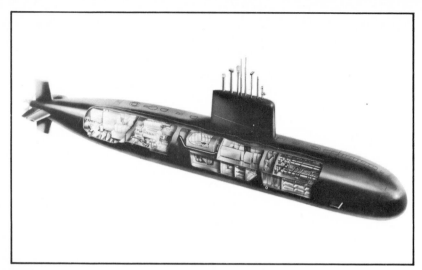

TYPE 2400 — AN ARTIST'S IMPRESSION

NEW CONVENTIONAL SUBMARINES.....

Despite the overall operational advantages of nuclear submarines there is still a requirement for conventional diesel electric submarines in a modern well balanced fleet. They are, relatively, cheap to build and can operate in the shallower waters around our coastline — as well as in the ocean deeps.

The type 2400 is long awaited by the Royal Navy — and the builders — hope for considerable overseas sales.

Principal Characteristics

Length	70m
Diameter of pressure hull	7.6m
Submerged displacement	2400 tons
Submerged speed	Over 20 knots
Complement	46

Weapons

6 torpedo tubes 12 reloads
Mines

Typical Mission

The Type 2400 provides 28 days patrol endurance after a transit of over 2500 nautical miles at normal cruising speeds.
Both the patrol duration and the tactical radius can be extended by reducing transit speed.
The large battery capacity, supported by a comprehensive air purification regeneration system, permits submerged periods of several days at a time.

SUBMARINE WEAPONS

Polaris away . . . .

POLARIS MISSILES: (See P.49) Sixteen Polaris A-3 missiles in addition to conventional torpedo weapons are carried by the four Royal Navy nuclear-powered 'Polaris' submarines. The 31 foot long missiles are fired from underwater. Each missile is housed in its own launch tube. The two-stage solid fuel rocket has an inertial guidance system to put it on course. At a pre-determined moment the guidance system shuts off the rocket motors and triggers separation of the re-entry body. The re-entry then follows a ballistic trajectory to the target. Polaris missiles are intercontinental ballistic nuclear weapons with a range of 2.500 miles and an accuracy measured in yards.

TORPEDOES

Torpedoes of various types still form the main armament of Royal Navy submarines. Even the four 'Polaris' submarines carry a combination of torpedoes as well as their deterrent missiles. Torpedoes are launched from underwater through special tubes against surface ships or submarines. Patrol submarines have six torpedo tubes forward and two aft. Nuclear-powered submarines carry all their torpedoes in their bow section. All Royal Navy submarines carry a large number of reloads.

MK 8 TORPEDO: Similar in many respects to the torpedoes of both World Wars, the Mk 8 is still a very effective anti-ship weapon. Fired in salvoes, its gyro-compass can be pre-set so that the attacking submarine does not have to point directly at its target. Once fired and on its course the submarine cannot influence its track. This 21-foot long diesel driven torpedo has a high-explosive warhead in common with all other types.

MK 20 TORPEDO: This is an electric-powered homing torpedo for use against fast moving escort ships. It contains its own acoustic homing device.

MK 24 TIGERFISH TORPEDO: One of the most advanced acoustic homing torpedoes in the world. Like the MK 23 it is initially wire guided but has its own homing device for the final stage of its attack. It can be regarded as an underwater guided missile for use against submarines and now also has an anti-surface ship capability.

MINES:

Ground and buoyant mines fitted with a variety of firing mechanisms can be carried by Patrol and Fleet submarines.

Torpedo fired!

A cliff face makes a handy target — imagine the result on a ship — rather than solid rock.

SUB HARPOON: (See outside back cover). Agreement was reached with the United States Government for the procurement of the Sub Harpoon submarine launched missile. Fired through a torpedo tube from underwater Sub Harpoon breaks the surface to become an air flight missile. It entered the service in the Royal Navy in the early 1980's and will provide the main anti-surface ship armament of the nuclear-powered submarine.

THE FLAG OFFICER SUBMARINES

The Flag Officer Submarines (FOSM) is the head of the Submarine Branch of the Royal Navy, the submarine type commander and the administrative authority for the submarine squadrons and bases.

While the Commander-in-Chief Fleet retains full command and control of all Royal Naval Submarines, operational command and control (with the exception of the Polaris submarines in their operational cycle) is delegated to FOSM.

FOSM, together with operations, warfare, engineering, training and administrative elements of his staff are located at Fleet Headquarters, Northwood, Middlesex. Other members of his staff are located at Fort Blockhouse, Gosport, Hants.

FOSM also has a NATO responsibility as Commander Submarines Eastern Atlantic (COMSUBEASTLANT).

SUBMARINE BASES

Royal Navy submarines operate from three main bases in the United Kingdom — HMS DOLPHIN at Gosport, Hants; HMS DEFIANCE at Plymouth, Devon; and HMS NEPTUNE at Faslane near Helensburgh in Scotland.

HMS DOLPHIN

HMS DOLPHIN is built around the site of the old fortifications known as Fort Blockhouse and is the "Alma Mater" of the Submarine Service. Today it is the headquarters of the First Submarine Squadron, comprising diesel-electric Patrol submarines.

Originally established as a military base by Henry VI in 1431, it was taken over by the Royal Navy in 1905 for the establishment of a "submarine boat station". The name DOLPHIN is taken from the old sail training ship of that name which was berthed alongside the fort from 1906-1923 as a depot ship for submarines.

Many additions and alterations have been made to the base — the most recent of which being the Submarine School Complex which was opened in 1977 and which will ensure the future of HMS DOLPHIN as a training establishment for submariners into the 21st Century.

Also at HMS DOLPHIN is the Submarine Memorial Museum and the "museum piece" submarine HMS ALLIANCE — which are open to the public.

The Queens Colours were presented to the Submarine Service by Her Majesty the Queen on 8 June 1959 and now hang in the wardroom at HMS DOLPHIN.

In recognition of the long association between the Submarine Service and the Borough of Gosport, the Honorary Freedom of the Borough of Gosport was conferred on the Submarine Service on July 7 1961.

HMS DOLPHIN — an unusual sight most of her 'brood' in harbour.

HMS DEFIANCE

A new submarine complex within the Devonport Naval Base provides the administrative headquarters of the Second Submarine Squadron — a "mixed bag" of diesel-electric powered Patrol submarines and nuclear powered Fleet submarines (including all the latest Swiftsure class Fleet submarines).

Major modern refitting facilities for diesel-electric and nuclear powered submarines have also been provided at Devonport. Other nuclear refitting facilities also exist at the Chatham and Rosyth Naval Bases. Portsmouth Naval Base is also able to refit Patrol submarines. Both Chatham and Portsmouth Naval bases however are due to be closed/run down in 1984.

HMS NEPTUNE

In December 1962 the Nassau Agreement was signed between the United States and the United Kingdom for the sale of "Polaris". The first British "Polaris" submarine was launched in September 1966 and began its first operational patrol in June 1968. In the meantime HMS NEPTUNE was built up primarily to support the Polaris programme and commissioned on August 10, 1967.

HMS NEPTUNE's role today is to support the four "Polaris" submarines of the Tenth Submarine Squadron; to support the nuclear-powered Fleet submarines and diesel-electric Patrol submarines of the Third Submarine Squadron; and to support submarines working up and visiting submarines and warships. It also provides support for naval personnel and their families — including accommodation, amenities and recreational facilities.

AN HISTORICAL BRIEF

332 BC	Alexander the Great reputed to have used some form of submersible vessel during the Siege of Tyre.
3rd Cent BC	Archimedes laid down the physical principles of displacement and submersion.
1580	The first recorded mention of a true submarine in the writings of an Englishman named William Bourne who published details of "a boate that may go under the water". Although his craft was not built, Bourne was the first to suggest how a submarine craft might realistically be made to dive and surface. Nevertheless the proposed craft was a crude wood and canvas design.
1578-1763	Records of 17 submarine inventions. Some were for peaceful purposes, such as recovering wrecks, but those which did have a military purpose did not influence naval warfare — primarily because most did not work and presented a greater danger to their crew than an enemy.
1620-1630	Cornelius van Drebbel built several submersible boats and records suggest that at least one worked. This was little more than a covered rowing boat but probably did manage to wallow beneath the Thames for a short distance.
1776	Twenty-nine years before the Battle of Trafalgar, David Bushnell, an American, constructed The Turtle, which resembled a large beer barrel. This was a one-man submarine propelled by muscle power. It was used to attack the British Fleet which was blockading New York Harbour during the American War of Independence. The operator, Ezra Lee, managed to propel the craft beneath the hull of the British flagship, Eagle, where he tried to screw an auger into the hull to which was attached an explosive charge primed by a clockwork detonator. The attack failed because Lee's auger struck a metal part of Eagle's hull. This was the first time a submarine had been used in anger.
1796	The American engineer Fulton designed a submarine. As America was no longer at war Fulton took his design to France where Napoleon gave him a grant to build the Nautilus. This was more mobile than Turtle and could be propelled on the surface by a sail. In spite of

	successful trials the French decided not to go ahead with this type of weapon, which they considered "dishonourable".
1804	Fulton brought his plans to England where they were examined by a Committee on which Pitt served. Pitt was enthusiastic but was crushed by a statement by one of Britain's greatest sailors, the Earl St Vincent, who said: "Pitt must be the greatest fool that ever existed to encourage a mode of war which those who command the sea do not want and which if successful will deprive them of it". This statement was to be the basis of British policy for almost 100 years thereafter.
1850	Bavarian William Bauer built the first iron submarine.
1863-1864	The Confederate Forces built several submarines to attack blockading Union ships during the American Civil War. One of these submarines made the first successful submarine attack in history against the frigate Hausatonic — sinking the Hausatonic but being itself also destroyed in the attack.
1620-1900	Between van Drebbel and the end of the 19th Century some 130 to 140 submarine designs were seriously considered and more than 50 others designed and built. By the turn of the 19th Century six navies owned a total of 10 submarines with 11 under construction. France led the field with 14 built or building. The United States had 2, of which "the Holland" was probably the most advanced in the world and even Italy, Portugal, Spain and Turkey had at least one craft each. Only in Britain was there discouragement.
1901	During exercises the French submarine Gustav Zede made a mock attack on the French Mediterranean Fleet after travelling 160 miles under her own power. She hit the French battleship Charles Martel with a dummy torpedo with complete surprise. The development of the Whitehead torpedo had been the most important development since the end of the American Civil War. Although not originally designed for submarines it led to their eventual success as warships.
	The Gustav Zede incident so shocked the British that an order for submarines of the American "Holland" design was made.
	On October 2, 1901 the Royal Navy's "Submarine No 1" was launched at Vickers' Barrow-in-Furness yard. The Royal Navy's Submarine Service was born.

57

"Submarine No 1" was an American Holland Type V built under licence. (This submarine was recently found on the seabed off Plymouth and is eventually to be displayed at the Submarine Museum Gosport.)

1901-1914   There was much initial opposition to the submarine. One admiral called it "underhand and damned un-English." Another suggested that all captured sub-mariners in wartime should be hanged as pirates.

1914-1918   By the outbreak of World War I the submarine had developed into an effective and efficient weapon, but was still considered primarily as a harbour defence vessel. The German U-boat U-9 put paid to that defensive concept when she sank 3 British cruisers at sea in less than an hour in the opening stages of the War.

Thereafter the submarine was used by both Germany and Britain in a blockading role. Indeed German wolf-packs attempted to cut off Britain from the outside world.

Between the   British submarines developed in strange ways. The K
Wars   Class was designed to have high surface speeds to keep pace with the Fleet. The M-Class was variously fitted with a 12″ gun and aircraft complete with hangar. In short, attempts were made to perfect the submarine for a surface fighting role, using its submersible capabilities primarily for getting into position secretively.

World War II   Germany's attempts to isolate Britain by U-boat warfare are well known. But in the Mediterranean British submarines played a vital role in cutting Rommel's supply lines and in the Pacific Allied submarines eventually dominated enemy surface forces.

Post War   The Germans had led the field in submarine development and by 1944 had perfected the schnorkel-fitted boat. After the War Britain adopted the "snort" system which enabled submarines to remain underwater for long periods. Development now concentrated on making the submarine fit for its true role — always under the water.

High Test Peroxide fuel was tried in experimental submarines to give high underwater speed and attempts were made to make the submarine quiet to avoid new detection techniques. The United States commissioned the nuclear-powered USS Nautilus in 1954 — the first true submarine.

1963	HMS DREADNOUGHT, Britain's first nuclear submarine was completed. The nuclear submarine can remain underwater for months at a time without even the necessity of having to come to periscope depth, and can travel at high underwater speeds.
Today	The Royal Navy now operates 13 nuclear-powered Fleet hunter attack submarines, and 16 diesel-electric powered Patrol submarines. These can be armed with homing and salvo torpedoes and submarine launched anti-ship air-flight guided missiles. Both classes are used in an anti-submarine and anti-ship role. In addition the Royal Navy has four nuclear-powered "Polaris" submarines which carry the Polaris intercontinental ballistic nuclear missiles which are Britain's contribution to the NATO strategic deterrent — a mighty advance from the days of Holland just 80 years ago.

The Latest   **HMS SPLENDID — sails from Gibraltar**

LIFE ON BOARD

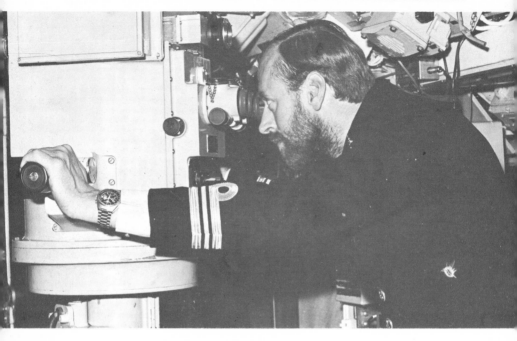

The Captain of a conventional submarine at the periscope.

Engine Room Ratings carry out maintainance routines on the main engines of a conventional submarine.

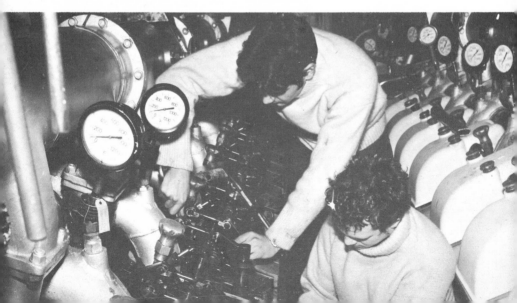

No ships wheel on a Nuclear boat — these submarines are "flown" using an aircraft type joystick.

The Forward Torpedo Compartment of a Nuclear boat.

WHAT THEY ARE UP AGAINST . . .
The Soviet Submarine Threat

Soviet Charlie Class Submarine

In the event of general war, it is believed that the Soviets see their navy fulfilling five basic functions in the overall war effort. Those are the provision of sea-based strategic nuclear strike forces as an assumed deterrent; the provision of forces to counter a Western seaborne nuclear strike against the Soviet Union launched from submarine and aircraft carriers; disruption of Western efforts to reinforce and re-supply Europe by sea; the sea control of the waters around the Soviet Union; and support for Soviet ground forces as required.

The submarine-launched strategic strike capability complements the land-based inter-continental ballistic missiles (ICBMs) which are vulnerable to attack since they are in silos whose locations are known. The oceans, on the other hand, offer a covert environment in which to deploy submarine-launched ballistic missiles (SLBMs). The submarine is constantly moving which increases difficulty of detection and subsequent destruction. The overwhelming majority of Soviet strategic missile submarines are nuclear powered, but some of the older diesel-powered missile-firing submarines of the Golf class are still retained in service, particularly where the depth of water is sufficient to enable them to fire their 700 nautical-mile-range missiles submerged. Their target area covers most of the UK, North East France and North Italy.

Since the late 1960s the strength of the SLBM has been greatly increased by the addition of 34 Yankee-class nuclear-powered ballistic-missile submarines (SSBNs) each carrying 16 missiles, each with a range of 1600 nautical miles, some of which have multiple warheads aimed at the same target area. Their patrol areas have to be in mid-Atlantic if

North America is to be within their missile range. In order to reduce SSBN vulnerablility still further and at the same time increase the target options available, further new classes of SSBN with increased missile ranges have been developed. The Delta 1 is larger than any NATO SSBN currently operating and later models of this class are even bigger. Each Delta-class SSBN carries 12 or 16 missiles with a range of over 4000 nautical miles while the latest SLBM being introduced is estimated to have multiple independently targeted re-entry vehicles (MIRV) capability. The increased range of these new missiles enables the Delta force, consisting of 25 submarines, to patrol in Soviet home waters, relatively safe from attack yet able simultaneously to cover targets in the USA, Europe and China. Over the past decade SSBNs have been completed at an average rate of one every two months! The USSR is reported to have begun building a new class of SSBN, which will be the largest ever built in the Soviet Union, and is expected to be comparable to the US Navy's Trident Class with its 24 SLBMs.

In 1968 the Soviets had about 40 ballistic missile-firing submarines of which only 14 were nuclear powered. By 1979 this figure had increased to about 90 of which about 70 were nuclear-powered, the newer boats carrying more powerful missiles with greater ranges. The number of SLBMs carried had risen from about 190 in 1968 to over 1000 by 1979.

The nuclear-powered hunter/killer submarines (SSNs) are likely to be reserved for distant areas where lack of air coverage could restrict Soviet surface involvment. There are about 40 SSNs of which about half are of the Victor class having a speed of over 30 knots and estimated to be the best Soviet anti-submarine platform currently operational. The diesel-powered hunter/killer submarines of the Foxtrot and Tango classes are likely to operate at choke points.

The Charlie-class nuclear-powered cruise missile-firing submarine (SSGN) with eight missiles was designed for the anti-strike carrier role. Although is effectiveness might apprear to be limited by the relatively short range of its missiles (30 miles), this very limitation implies that it would need no external assistance in locking the weapons on their targets. NATO carriers are also likely to be the target of longer-range cruise missiles carried by submarines of the Echo II and Juliet classes.

The impact of the Soviet building and modernisation programme can be seen by looking at the major threat to the North Atlantic — the Northern Fleet. The following table illustrates its greatly increased capability since 1968.

	1968	1979
Submarines (approx)	194	195
(nuclear powered - approx)	44	104

It is noteworthy that these increases have largely been concentrated in the more powerful nuclear-powered vessels at the expense of the less-effective units.

Index

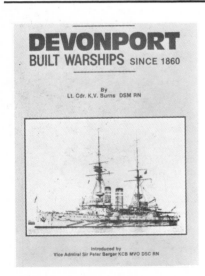

Devonport Built Warships Since 1860
By Lt Cdr K. V. Burns D.S.M., R.N.
An extremely well produced book (so said ITV) by the former Plymouth Naval History Librarian. Over 60 photographs illustrate a book packed with information. We thought it would only sell in Plymouth but orders have come in from around the world.
£2.30

Falklands — Task Force Portfolio
Quite simply a superb photographic record of this magnificent force. Large format 112 pages — nearly 200 photographs.

£4.95 inc post